The Really **Wild Life of Snakes**™

PIT VIPERS

DOUG WECHSLER
ACADEMY OF NATURAL SCIENCES

The Rosen Publishing Group's

PowerKids Press™
New York

For Mr. Nodell and Mrs. Ward

About the Author
Wildlife biologist, ornithologist, and photographer Doug Wechsler has studied birds, snakes, frogs, and other wildlife around the world. Doug Wechsler works at The Academy of Natural Sciences of Philadelphia, a natural history museum. As part of his job, he travels to rain forests and remote parts of the world to take pictures of birds. He has taken part in expeditions to Ecuador, the Philippines, Borneo, Cuba, Cameroon, and many other countries.

Published in 2001 by The Rosen Publishing Group, Inc.
29 East 21st Street, New York, NY 10010

First Edition

Book Design: Michael de Guzman

Photo Credits: pp. 4, 7, 15, 16, 19, 20, 22 © Doug Wechsler; p. 8 © Joe McDonald/Animals Animals; p. 11 © Breck P. Kent/Animals Animals; p. 12 © C. C. Lockwood/Animals Animals.

Wechsler, Doug.
    Pit vipers / Doug Wechsler.—1st ed.
      p. cm.— (The really wild life of snakes)
    Includes bibliographical references (p.).
    ISBN 0-8239-5605-9 (alk. paper)
    1. Pit vipers—Juvenile literature. [1. Pit vipers. 2. Snakes.] I. Title.

  QL666.O69 W43 2000
  597.96'3—dc21   00-035981

Manufactured in the United States of America

CONTENTS

DOUG SAYS

THERE ARE 157 SPECIES OF PIT VIPERS IN THE WORLD. SOUTH AMERICA HAS THE MOST SPECIES OF PIT VIPERS.

WHAT IS A PIT VIPER?

Pit vipers are the only snakes with a single pair of **pits** on their faces. The pits are little holes that sense heat. Pit vipers are a group of **venomous** snakes found in North and South America and in Southeast Asia. All **species** of pit vipers are dangerous and many are deadly. Many have skins with beautiful patterns. Pit vipers from North America include copperheads, cottonmouths, and many kinds of rattlesnakes. All pit vipers have a pair of moveable **fangs**. The fangs are special hollow teeth used for shooting poison into **prey** and enemies.

Nearly all pit vipers give birth to live young. Only a few species, such as the bushmaster, lay eggs.

This slender hog-nosed pit viper lives in Costa Rica in Central America. Pit vipers can be found in a wide range of areas, from deserts to rain forests.

THE PITS

Imagine if you could tell a person was three feet (91 cm) away just by feeling the warmth of his or her body. That is what the pit viper's pits can do. The pits are special sense organs that feel heat. Like eyes, pits come in pairs. There is one on each side of a pit viper's face, between the eye and the nostril. The little holes point forward toward the prey. Having two pits helps the snake tell just how far away the prey or enemy is. Using the information from its pits, a pit viper can strike at a mouse two feet (60 cm) away in the dark.

A close view of this copperhead in Texas shows one of its pits. The pit organ senses heat to aid the snake in finding warm-blooded prey.

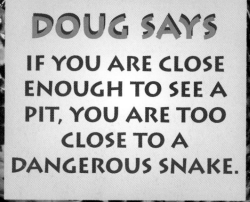

DOUG SAYS
IF YOU ARE CLOSE
ENOUGH TO SEE A
PIT, YOU ARE TOO
CLOSE TO A
DANGEROUS SNAKE.

DOUG SAYS

CERTAIN TYPES OF VENOM CAN ALSO BE USED TO MAKE MEDICINE.

VIPER VENOM

Venom is the poison in an animal's bite or sting. Pit vipers have special venom glands in the backs of their mouths where the venom is made. Pit viper venom is a **chemical** punch. It is a mix of many different nasty chemicals. Each chemical does something awful to the **victim**. One makes the animal bleed, one stops it from breathing, and one starts to **digest** the animal even before it has been eaten. Each pit viper has its own special mix of chemicals. One pit viper from China is called the hundred-pace viper. It is said that if it bites you, that is how many paces, or steps, you take before you die.

This close view of the fangs of an eastern diamondback rattlesnake shows a drop of venom. The snake's venom will begin to digest prey before it gets swallowed.

FUN FACTS ABOUT FANGS

Fangs are hollow teeth. The poison travels through the fangs to get beneath the skin of a victim. Behind the fangs are the venom **sacs**. These sacs store the venom made in the venom glands. When the pit viper's mouth is closed, the fangs are folded back into the mouth. At the moment a pit viper strikes, it moves its fangs forward. As the fangs sink into the victim's skin, the venom sacs are squeezed. The poison shoots through the hollow fangs into the victim.

An eastern diamondback rattlesnake uses its fangs to move a mouse and its tail into the snake's mouth.

COTTONMOUTHS

All pit vipers swim, but only one is at home in the water. The cottonmouth lives in swamps, rivers, and lakes in the southeastern United States. It feeds both on the shore and in the water. It will eat almost any small animal. Fish, frogs, snakes, and birds are its usual diet. It also eats small turtles, insects, and **carrion**. Where does the name cottonmouth come from? Anyone who sees an angry cottonmouth will know. The inside of its mouth is white. The white mouth acts as a threat. The sight of the opened mouth is enough to scare away most enemies. This saves the cottonmouth the trouble of having to bite. If a cottonmouth bites an enemy, it loses valuable venom that it can use to get food.

This western cottonmouth is at home in a swamp in Louisiana. Cottonmouths are also known as water moccasins.

HIDDEN COPPERHEADS

Copperheads, like most pit vipers, would rather hide than fight. No snake can hide better than a copperhead. It hides among the dead leaves in the forests of the eastern United States. Copperheads are colored like dead leaves. They rarely bite if they are not threatened. When they are attacked, they strike quickly. Copperheads are dangerous, but they hardly ever kill anyone.

In the Appalachian Mountains, copperheads spend the winter in dens. The dens are in spaces between rocks, deep underground in a hillside. They often share dens with timber rattlesnakes.

The patterns of copperheads vary from place to place. All copperheads blend in well among dead leaves.

DOUG SAYS

THE LARGEST PIT VIPER IS THE BUSHMASTER. IT LIVES IN UNDISTURBED RAIN FORESTS OF CENTRAL AND SOUTH AMERICA. THE RECORD SIZE IS JUST OVER 12 FEET (3.65 M).

PIT VIPERS IN THE TREES

The most beautiful pit vipers live in trees and bushes. They are **arboreal**. Arboreal pit vipers live in Central and South America and Southeast Asia. Many are green, so they can blend in with the leaves. A few are bluish or bright yellow. Some arboreal pit vipers have **prehensile** tails, like monkeys. These tails are strong. They wrap around branches to safely hold the snakes high above the ground.

Young arboreal pit vipers usually eat frogs and lizards. As they get older and larger, they start to eat birds and small mammals.

An aboreal pit viper in Malaysia moves along the branch of a tree. These pit vipers blend in with the leaves of trees.

DEFENSE

Even though pit vipers are venomous, they have plenty of **predators**. Hawks, owls, and toucans eat pit vipers. Even some snakes, like indigo snakes and king snakes, snack on pit vipers. A pit viper's first line of defense is its **camouflage**. Many pit vipers have blotchy skin patterns. They blend in perfectly with dry leaves.

If camouflage does not work, the snake may threaten an enemy by moving into a striking position. Rattlesnakes will rattle. Some other pit vipers vibrate their tails to make warning sounds in the dry leaves. Most pit vipers will only strike if they have to defend themselves. At least one pit viper, the cantil of Costa Rica, can play dead when threatened.

If their camouflage does not keep enemies away, cantils, like this one in Costa Rica, play dead.

INDEX

WEB SITES

To learn more about pit vipers, check out these Web sites:

http://www.ncweb.com/users/gostanek
http://www.stetson.edu/departments/biology/pigpage.html

GLOSSARY

arboreal (ar-BOR-ee-uhl) Living in trees.

camouflage (CAM-oh-flahj) To hide by a pattern that matches one's background.

carrion (KEHR-ee-un) Dead, rotting flesh of animals.

chemical (KEH-mih-kul) A substance that can be mixed with other substances to cause reactions.

digest (dy-JEST) When a body breaks down the food it eats for energy.

fangs (FANGZ) Hollow teeth that inject venom.

hibernate (HY-bur-nayt) To spend the winter in a deep sleep.

pits (PITS) Sense organs on the face of a snake that detect heat. On pit vipers, the pits are shallow holes between the eye and the nostril.

predators (PREH-duh-terz) Animals that kill other animals for food.

prehensile (pree-HEN-sul) Used for grasping by wrapping around. Tails of spider monkeys, tree boas, and opossums are prehensile.

prey (PRAY) An animal that is eaten by another animal for food.

sacs (SAKS) Pouchlike parts in a plant or animal.

species (SPEE-sheez) A single kind of plant or animal. For example, all people are one species.

terciopelo (tar-see-oh-PAY-lo) A large, dangerous pit viper common in Central America. It is sometimes known as a fer-de-lance.

venom (VEN-um) A poison passed by one animal into another through a bite or sting.

venomous (VEN-um-us) Having a poisonous bite.

victim (VIK-tim) A person or animal that is harmed or killed.

THE BEST-KNOWN PIT VIPER

Rattlesnakes are the best known of all pit vipers. When enemies come too close to them, these snakes often warn them with the rattles on their tails. No other snake has a rattle. The rattle is made of a row of dried scalelike parts. A new part of the rattle is added each time the snake sheds its skin. The rattle's sound scares off enemies.

Like copperheads, many rattlesnakes spend winters in dens. On warm spring days, they warm themselves on rocks outside the dens. Each winter they return to the same den to **hibernate**. Pit vipers eat lots of rats and mice. These pests can spread diseases or eat our food. By helping rattlesnakes survive, we help ourselves stay free of these pests.

THE MOST DANGEROUS PIT VIPER

No snake is more feared in Central America than the **terciopelo**. It is sometimes called a fer-de-lance. The terciopelo and its relatives are the most dangerous snakes in Central and South America. Anyone living in the countryside there can tell you stories about people who were bitten. What makes terciopelos so dangerous? They blend in with the dead leaves on the ground. This makes them hard to see. They often do not flee from people, like most snakes. They are quick to strike and they like brushy areas around farms. A four-foot (1.2-m) terciopelo has fangs over an inch (2.5 cm) long. These fangs can put lots of deadly venom into a victim.

This terciopelo in Costa Rica is hard to see when it hides in dead leaves. Terciopelos cause more injuries and deaths in Central America than any other snake.

PYTHON LEGS

In the days of *Stegosaurus*, 150 million years ago, the **ancestors** of snakes had legs. Snakes' ancestors were much like lizards. By about 100 million years ago, ancestors of today's snakes were probably living mostly underground. They had only tiny legs by this time. Legs get in the way of an animal that lives underground and pushes through the soil. Today most snakes have no legs, but pythons still have two tiny legs called spurs. The spurs look like sharp, little pegs. They are found on the sides of the body where the tail begins. Male pythons use their spurs to tickle the females during **courtship**.

Snakes no longer have the legs their ancestors had. Pythons still have tiny back legs, called spurs. Males usually have spurs that are more developed than the ones on females.

The reticulated python holds the record for being the world's longest snake. The longest reticulated python ever measured was just over 32 feet (9.8 m) long. Imagine this python in a school bus **aisle**. If its tail touched the back, its head would almost touch the white line near the driver at the front of the bus. Giant snakes this size are extremely rare. Most adult pythons do not grow over 16 feet (4.9 m) long.

The oldest known snake was a ball python that lived in the Philadelphia Zoo. It lived in the zoo for 47 years. It was already a young adult when it arrived at the zoo, so it probably lived to be about 50 years old.

This is a ball python. Ball pythons live in Africa. They are called ball pythons because they wrap themselves up into a ball shape to protect themselves from enemies.

▷

DOUG SAYS

PYTHONS HAVE CLOSE TO 400 BACK BONES.

DOUG SAYS

THE DIAMOND PYTHON IS ONE OF THE FEW SNAKES THAT BUILDS A NEST. IT PUSHES DEAD LEAVES TOGETHER ON THE GROUND AND CRAWLS BENEATH THEM.

Some snakes give birth to live baby snakes that are not hatched from eggs. Pythons, though, lay eggs. Large pythons lay a lot of eggs. A large reticulated python can lay more than 60 eggs at a time. The smallest python, the dwarf python, lays only two to five eggs at a time. A mother python guards her eggs, unlike most other snakes. She stays **coiled** around the eggs for about two months until they hatch. Burmese pythons and scrub pythons **incubate** their eggs. The mother keeps the eggs warm by wrapping her body around them and shivering. The shivering warms her body, and her body then warms the eggs. Pythons are the only snakes that warm their eggs this way.

A Burmese python egg hatches after being incubated for two months. The young python will soon go off on its own.

13

Pythons are a dentist's dream. A python can have as many as 150 teeth in its mouth. All the teeth are the same shape. Each tooth is curved toward the back of the mouth. The teeth in the front are larger than the teeth in the back. When a python grabs its prey, it gets a good grip with all of those teeth. After the python kills its prey, the curved teeth help guide the prey down the python's throat. Pythons lose their teeth easily. Even before a tooth falls out, another tooth is ready to take its place.

A python may have as many as 150 teeth in its mouth. If a tooth falls out, another one is right there waiting to replace it.

FEEDING

A python grabs its prey with its toothy mouth. Then it quickly wraps its long body around the prey. The python constricts to stop the prey from breathing. Once the prey is dead, the python will swallow it headfirst. A python can open its jaws very wide. The whole jaw stretches away from the skull. This lets it swallow things that seem too wide to fit inside the python's body.

Pythons are patient when looking for food. An Angolan python might wait for days by a spring to feed on doves that come to drink. A diamond python in Australia may spend a week in a tree waiting to **ambush** an opossum that climbs up the tree.

◁ *This reticulated python can open its mouth very wide. That way it can swallow prey that is fatter than its own body.*

PYTHONS EAT PIGS

Pythons do not have to eat very often. They eat very large meals that fill them up for a long time. The largest pythons eat small pigs, deer, antelope, and even leopards. A 16-foot (4.9-m) African rock python once ate a 130-pound (59-kg) **impala**. An impala is a kind of antelope that looks like a deer. A 24-foot (7.3-m) reticulated python can eat a 120-pound (54.4-kg) pig. When a python eats a pig, it may not feed again for months. Once an African rock python waited two and a half years between meals. Of course small pythons do not eat such huge animals.

The African rock python shown here can grow up to 24.6 feet (7.5 m) long.

▷

DOUG SAYS

MOST SNAKES HAVE
ONLY ONE LUNG
FOR BREATHING,
BUT PYTHONS
HAVE TWO.

DOUG SAYS

WITHIN FOUR YEARS PEOPLE IN THE COUNTRIES OF INDONESIA AND THAILAND SOLD 300,000 PYTHON SKINS TO PEOPLE IN OTHER COUNTRIES.

PIGS EAT PYTHONS, TOO

Pythons have many enemies. Small pythons are attacked by just about any medium-sized meat-eating animal. Wild pigs, eagles, baboons, and king cobras are a few python **predators**. The bigger a python grows, the smaller its enemy list gets. Monster-sized pythons have to watch out for crocodiles, tigers, and hyenas. Many people are also enemies of pythons. Other people kill them for food. Some people sell python skins to make shoes, purses, and other items. In some places, blood pythons and ball pythons have become rare because they are caught and sold as pets. Pythons could use more human friends.

In some areas blood pythons, like the one pictured here, have become rare in the wild. This is because they are often caught and sold as pets.

PYTHONS, POULTRY, AND PEOPLE?

Pythons are fond of eating **poultry**. Pythons also eat rats and other pesky animals. In Asia some pythons live at the edges of cities. They sometimes dine on cats and dogs.

Pythons rarely attack people. The only people likely to get bitten are those who try to capture a python. A python will defend itself by biting if it is cornered. It is dangerous to pick up a huge python alone, even if it is tame. A big python is very powerful. If it starts to squeeze, it could be hard for the person to escape without help. Many people eat pythons, but pythons almost never eat people.

GLOSSARY

aisle (EY-el) A narrow space for walking between rows of seats.

ambush (AM-bush) To attack by surprise from a hiding place.

ancestors (AN-ses-turz) Relatives who lived long ago.

camouflaged (KA-muh-flajd) When an animal is blended into its surroundings because of the color or pattern of its feathers, fur, or skin.

coiled (KOYLD) Wound into a ring.

constrictors (kun-STRICKT-urs) Snakes that kill their prey by coiling their bodies around the prey and squeezing.

courtship (KORT-ship) The period of activity before a male and female join together to make babies.

impala (im-PAHL-ah) A medium-sized antelope from Africa.

incubate (IN-kyoo-bayt) To keep eggs warm, usually using body temperature.

poultry (POL-tree) Birds, such as chickens, ducks, and turkeys, raised for their meat or eggs.

predators (PREH-duh-ters) Animals that kill other animals for food.

prey (PRAY) An animal that is eaten by another animal for food.

reticulated (reh-TIH-kyoo-lay-ted) Having a pattern that looks like a net.

Stegosaurus (steh-geh-SOR-us) A very large plant-eating dinosaur with bony plates and spikes along its back and tail.

stout (STOWT) Having a thick body.

tropics (TRAH-piks) The warm parts of the earth that are near the equator.

23

INDEX

WEB SITES

To learn more about pythons, check out these Web sites:

http://www.amnh.org/Exhibition/Endangered/python/python.html
http://www.nature.ca/notebooks/english/python.htm
http://www.perthzoo.wa.gov.au/woma.html